MA+HS
IS EVERYWHERE

WHAT ARE THE CHANCES?

Probability, statistics, **ratios** and **proportions**

Rob Colson

Acknowledgments and Picture credits

Published Great Britain in 2018 by
The Watts Publishing Group

Copyright © The Watts Publishing Group,
2016

Series editor: Sarah Peutrill

Produced by Tall Tree Ltd
Design: Ben Ruocco
Consultants: Hilary Koll and Steve Mills

ISBN: 978 1 4451 4948 6

Printed in China

MIX
Paper from
responsible sources
FSC
www.fsc.org
FSC® C104740

Franklin Watts
An imprint of
Hachette Children's Group
Part of The Watts Publishing Group
Carmelite House
50 Victoria Embankment
London EC4Y 0DZ

An Hachette UK Company
www.hachette.co.uk

www.franklinwatts.co.uk

Picture credits:
t-top, b-bottom, l-left, r-right, c-centre,
front cover-fc, back cover-bc
All images courtesy of Dreamstime.com,
unless indicated:
Inside front Atman; fc, bc Pablo631; fcbl
Jennifer Bray; bcc Rawpixelimages;
1c, 9c, 28b Ronalds Stikans; 4tl
lineartestpilot/shutterstock.com; 4cr
Davulcu; 4b Svanhorn4245; fccr, 5b
Alexlmx; 4c Tigatelu; 7 Tijanap; bctl, 7b,
31t Dannyphoto80; 8c, 23t Mexrix; 8tb,
28t Cowpland; fccl, Valeriy Kachaev;
10t Zentilia; 11b Gorbelabda; fctr, 12l
Ronstik; 13t Olgacov; 13b Nikolais; fctc,
14t Hamsterman; 14tc Ha4ipuri; 14b
Basheeradesigns; 16t Jenny Lipets-
michaeli; 16b Rawpixelimages; 18l
Evgenii Naumov; 19 Cameramannz;
fctc, 20b Gilotyna; 21t Larryrains; 22b
Andreadonetti; 22br Paul Michael Hughes;
23cl NASA, fcbr, 23cr Macrovector; 24c
Ayo88; 26b Viteethumb; bctr, 27t Huseyin
Bas; 29r Binkski; 32t Stylephotographs

Luck of the draw

Probability is a calculation of the chance that something will happen. Also known as odds, probability shows how often you could expect something to happen if you repeated it again and again. For example, you could expect to be struck by lightning once every 900,000 years.

Probable or possible?

The chance of something happening can be expressed by a number between 0 and 1, where 0 means it will never happen and 1 means it will happen every time. A chance of $1/2$ is called evens – it is likely to happen exactly half the time.

Odds of being struck by lightning next year

900,000 to 1

Odds of being dealt four of a kind in poker

4,161 to 1

Odds of a mother having identical twins

285 to 1

Odds of throwing two sixes with a pair of dice

36 to 1

"You grow another nose."

"Tossing a coin and getting heads."

"Christmas Day is on the 25th of December."

0
(impossible)

½
(evens)

1
(certain)

"Winning the lottery jackpot."

"It will rain during Wimbledon fortnight."

Winning numbers

In some lotteries, players choose six different numbers between 1 and 49. To win the jackpot, these numbers must match six numbers drawn at random. There are 13,983,816 possible combinations of numbers, but only one can win. So the odds of winning are:

13,983,815 to 1

Out of 100

The per cent symbol means 'out of a hundred'. It is a way of expressing a fraction in terms of parts per one hundred.

1	2	3	4	5	6	7	8	9	10
11	12	13	14	15	16	17	18	19	20
21	22	23	24	25	26	27	28	29	30
31	32	33	34	35	36	37	38	39	40
41	42	43	44	45	46	47	48	49	50
51	52	53	54	55	56	57	58	59	60
61	62	63	64	65	66	67	68	69	70
71	72	73	74	75	76	77	78	79	80
81	82	83	84	85	86	87	88	89	90
91	92	93	94	95	96	97	98	99	100

One per cent is one part in 100. Here one square in 100 is coloured red.

100% of the squares have a white outline.

25 of these 50 squares are coloured green, which is 50 per cent.

1	2	3	4	5
6	7	8	9	10
11	12	13	14	15
16	17	18	19	20
21	22	23	24	25
26	27	28	29	30
31	32	33	34	35
36	37	38	39	40
41	42	43	44	45
46	47	48	49	50

Percentages as fractions and decimals

Percentages as fractions

When we say 20 per cent, what we mean is the fraction

$$\frac{20}{100}$$

Simplifying the fraction, $\frac{20}{100}$ can also be expressed as $\frac{1}{5}$.

Percentages as decimals

To write a percentage as a decimal, you **divide the number** by 100 by moving the digits two places to the right:

20.00% becomes 0.20

Borrowers beware!

People who borrow money from a bank are charged interest. This is additional money that you must pay back on top of the amount borrowed. If you don't pay the money back, the interest can mount up. This is due to something called **compound interest**, where interest is charged on the interest!

For example, if you borrow **£100** at an interest rate charged at **10%** at the end of each year, you will owe **£110** after the first year.

100 + (100 × 10%) = 110

If you think that after 10 years you'll owe £200, you've forgotten the power of compound interest.

In the second year, you are charged interest on £110, not £100. At the end of the second year, you will owe

£121
110 + (110 × 10%) = 121

At the end of the third year, you will owe

£133.10
121 + (121 × 10%) = 133.1

After 10 years, you will owe

£259.37

"I owe how much?"

Sales talk

Shops advertise sales in a way that makes the deal seem better than it is. 'Buy one, get one half price' sounds impressive, but what it really means is that you get **25%** off the price of each item when you buy two. Nothing is 'half price' in that deal – everything is **75%** of the price.

£1 + £0.50
= £1.50
= 75% × £2

7

Rolling the dice

A standard die has six sides with between one and six dots on each side. The chance of rolling any particular number is 1 divided by the number of sides, or $1/6$.

Two dice

Working out the probability of different scores with two dice is more complicated. Some scores are more likely than others. To see this, think about rolling the same die twice. Combining the scores of each roll gives possible scores of 2 to 12. There are 36 possible combinations, many of which give the same score.

Score from dice two

Score from dice one

	1	2	3	4	5	6
1	2	3	4	5	6	7
2	3	4	5	6	7	8
3	4	5	6	7	8	9
4	5	6	7	8	9	10
5	6	7	8	9	10	11
6	7	8	9	10	11	12

The most likely score is 7. There are 6 different possible ways of scoring 7, which gives a probability of $6/36$, or $1/6$. By contrast, there is just one way to score 12: rolling a 6 then another 6. That gives a probability of $1/36$. Can you work out the probability of scoring 3?

Doubles?

The chance of throwing a double (the same number twice) is the same as the chance of throwing a particular number once: whichever number you throw first, you need that number on the second throw. The chance of that happening is $1/6$. The six possible doubles are in the black squares across the diagonal in the chart above.

The Game of Pig

The Game of Pig is a simple dice game for two players that involves working out risk. All you need to play is a die. Player 1 rolls the die and can keep rolling until they decide to 'hold' or they roll a 1. If they hold, they keep the score of their rolls added together, but if they roll a 1, they score zero. Then it is player 2's turn. The first player to 100 is the winner. So, for instance, if Ann rolls 4–5–1, she scores zero, or 'pig', and it is then Bob's turn. If Bob then rolls 6–3 and holds, he scores 9, and it's Ann's turn again.

"Aarrgghh, pig."

"Woo hoo, 5 then 6."

Strategies when playing Pig

Each time you roll the die, there's a $1/6$ chance that you'll roll a 1. How many times would you risk it to get yourself a greater score? Mathematicians study games like this to explore probability and risk. There are three different factors that you need to weigh up: the total for your turn, your score before your turn and your opponent's score. If you're winning, you might take fewer risks, but if your opponent is close to 100, you may have little choice but to go for it.

It's a lottery

In many national lotteries, the jackpot is several million pounds. To win the money, players must match their choice of six numbers between 1 and 49 to the numbers drawn.

Jackpot!

One way to work out the odds of winning the jackpot is to look at each choice by turn. The first choice has a $^6/_{49}$ chance of being one of the six numbers. If it's there, then the second choice has a $^5/_{48}$ chance. If that's there, the third choice has a $^4/_{47}$ chance. The final choice has just a $^1/_{44}$ chance of being there.

So the odds of winning are:

$$^6/_{49} \times {}^5/_{48} \times {}^4/_{47} \times {}^3/_{46} \times {}^2/_{45} \times {}^1/_{44} = {}^{720}/_{10,068,347,520}$$

Simplifying, that works out at odds of

$$^1/_{13,983,816}$$

to win the jackpot.

Favourite numbers

Each number has the same chance of coming up, so the odds of the numbers being 1, 2, 3, 4, 5 and 6 are the same as the odds for 3, 11, 19, 21, 36 and 43. However, if people choose numbers that others don't choose, they won't have to share the pot if they win. And it turns out that we're far from random in our selections.

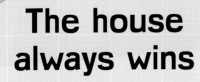

The house always wins

There is always one winner every week in the lottery, and that is the lottery itself. National lotteries are set up to make money for good causes. To guarantee a profit, the lottery makes sure that the total payout each week is less than the total earned in ticket sales. In the UK national lottery, the payout is about **45 per cent**, meaning that **55 per cent** of the price of a ticket goes to the lottery, not to the winners. **The only way to guarantee a win in the lottery is to run one!**

Unlucky!

Spare a thought for a woman in the USA who played both the Maryland and Delaware state lotteries one week in 1990. Both sets of numbers came up. Unfortunately for her, her Maryland numbers came up in Delaware and her Delaware numbers came up in Maryland, so she didn't win a penny!

Avoiding the obvious:

1 Avoid low numbers – lots of people choose birthdays, but there are only 31 days in any month, so the numbers 32–49 are less popular.

2 Avoid 3 and 7 in particular – these are many people's favourites, as is any number ending in a 7.

3 13 is thought unlucky by some, which is why it could prove very profitable for others.

4 The least popular number of all is 34. But keep that fact a secret – if too many people find out, it might just change!

Coins and cards

> "Flipping eck, I don't like heights."

Heads or tails

The toss of a coin represents an evens chance of each outcome: it's either a head or a tail. Each toss is independent, which means that you're not more likely to get a tail this time just because you got a head last time.

Double or quits?

The chance of getting every call wrong halves with each toss. So there is a $1/2$ chance of getting one wrong, $1/4$ chance of getting two out of two wrong, $1/8$ chance of getting three out of three wrong, and $1/16$ chance of getting four out of four wrong. When betting on the toss of a coin, it may be worth asking 'Double or quits?' That means asking to have another toss. If someone asks it enough times, they're likely to come out quits.

But beware:
Unlikely things do still happen sometimes – each time, they're trading a chance of coming out even with a chance of a bigger loss. They'd better have deep pockets!

Is it a fair toss?

After tossing a fair coin five times and coming up with five heads, the chance of a sixth head is still $1/2$.

However, what if someone were to come up with 200 heads in a row?

The chance of 200 heads in a row is $1/2^{200}$ (2^{200} is 2 multiplied by 2 200 times). You're more likely to win the lottery every week for two months straight. When something this unlikely happens, you need to question your assumptions. You have assumed it is a fair coin, but is it really? If someone throws 200 heads in a row, ask to have a look at the coin. It probably has heads on both sides.

"Smells like cheating to me!"

Pick a card

Card players need to know what the chances are of picking certain cards. A standard deck has 52 cards, so the chance of being dealt any one card is $1/52$. There are four aces, so the chance of being dealt an ace is $4/52$, or $1/13$.

What are the chances of being dealt two aces as your first cards?

Here you need to remember that after the first choice, there are now only 51 cards left and only three of them are aces. The chance of the second card being an ace is $3/51$, or $1/17$. Multiplying the chances together, you get $1/13 \times 1/17 = 1/221$

Taking an average

An average is a way of expressing the central value of a set of values. Mathematicians use several different ways of calculating an average.

How tall?

The heights (in metres) of seven children in a class are as follows.

1.4, 1.8, 1.2, 1.9, 1.7, 1.4, 1.6

To calculate the **mean average height**, you add up all the heights and divide by the number of children.

$$1.4 + 1.8 + 1.2 + 1.9 + 1.7 + 1.4 + 1.6 = 11 \div 7 = 1.57$$

To calculate the **median height**, you line the heights up in order and take the middle value:

1.2, 1.4, 1.4, 1.6, 1.7, 1.8, 1.9

So the **median height** is **1.6**

The **mode** is the most common height. There are two children who are **1.4 m** in height, so the mode is **1.4**.
The **range** is the difference between the tallest and the shortest. Here, the range is:

1.9 − 1.2 = 0.7

2 metres

1.5 metres

1 metre

0.5 metres

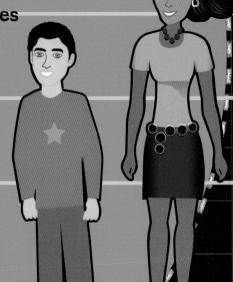

A closer shave?

A study that followed more than 2,000 men over 20 years found that men who shaved every day lived longer, on average, than men who did not shave every day. The study was reported in the press as having found a link between shaving and a longer life. However, it does not mean that men should shave more often for their health. It only means that men who don't look after their health are also less likely to shave. As a rule, scientists say that

correlation
(things happening together) does not necessarily mean

causation
(one of the things causes the other). It could be that both things are caused by something else entirely.

Resetting the median

IQ scores rank us according to our ability to answer questions in tests. A score of 100 is set to be the median score for the whole population. However, we are getting better at IQ tests, and every few years, the scale has to be re-set – an IQ score of 100 today needs a much higher mark than it needed 50 years ago. Scientists argue over why this is. Are we getting smarter, or are we just getting better at doing tests?

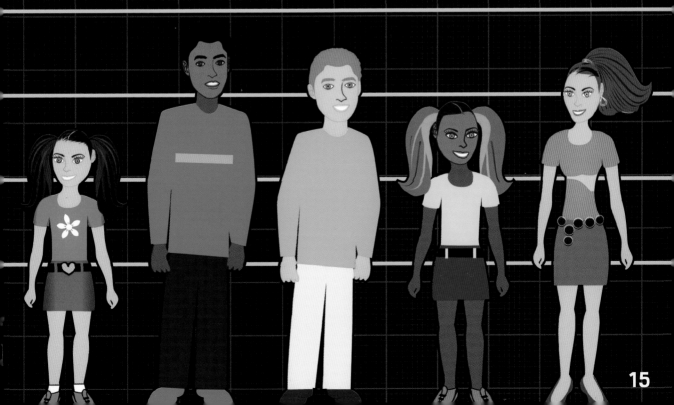

Not what it seems

We often have a feel for how likely something is. For instance, you can have a good sense that throwing ten 6s in a row with a fair die is unlikely before working out the exact odds. But sometimes we can be fooled. Here is a mind-twisting example.

The blood test

A blood test for a certain disease gives two results:

positive means you have the disease,

negative means you don't have the disease.

The test is known to be **99 per cent** accurate. This means that the test gives the wrong result once every 100 tests.

We also know that the disease is found on average in **1 person** out of every **10,000**.

You take the test and the result is positive. But what are the chances that you actually have the disease?

How worried should you be?

The answer might surprise you: you have only about a **1 per cent** chance of having the disease. There is a **99 per cent** chance that the test was wrong and you do not have it!

To see why this is, imagine performing the test on

10,000 people.

On average, just one of the people will have the disease. However, 1/100 of 10,000 tests will produce false results:

$$^1/_{100} \times 10,000 = 100$$

So there are, on average, **100 false results** in every **10,000 tests**. Where the test should have identified **one person** with the disease, it in fact came up with about **100 names**. There's about a **99 per cent** chance that your name will be one of those mistakes.

"Oh no, it's me isn't it?"

This result is known as a **'false positive'**, and it is the reason doctors often perform tests several times to confirm a diagnosis.

How to mislead with statistics

When you hear the word 'average', be careful that you know which average is being used. The average amount of something per person and the amount an average person has may be two very different things.

Bad drivers

About 80 per cent of people consider themselves to be above average drivers. However, using the median average, exactly 50 per cent of drivers must be below average! At least 30 per cent of people must be wrong.

"**Hey, it wasn't my fault!**"

Average apples

Here is a list of the number of apples produced by six people's gardens in a year.

Smith	350
Cox	7,000
Bramley	0
Jones	0
Pippin	150
Khan	200
Lambourne	0

How hot?

In a test, four diners are asked to rank three peppers by how hot they taste, with the hottest ranked 3rd. Here are the results:

	Pepper 1	Pepper 2	Pepper 3
Yasmin	3	1	2
Toby	3	2	1
Jemma	3	1	2
Folarin	3	2	1

The mean scores for each pepper from these results are as follows:

	Pepper 1	Pepper 2	Pepper 3
	3	1.5	1.5

Does that make Pepper 1 twice as hot as Peppers 2 and 3?

Everyone agrees that **Pepper 1** is the **hottest**, so it is probably much hotter than **Pepper 2** or **3**. It may be that it is **1,000 times hotter**. As these are rankings only, the **mean average** is only the **mean ranking**, and tells us nothing about how hot the peppers actually are.

The **mean** number of apples per garden is

1,100

However, the **median** is just

150

and the **mode** is

0

It turns out that the Coxes have a whole orchard in their garden, the Smiths, Pippins and Khans have one tree each, and everyone else has no tree at all.

So which do you think is the 'average' garden?

To avoid this kind of distortion, mean averages are sometimes taken with the biggest and lowest numbers removed. Taking away the Coxes and one of the zero gardens, you get a much more sensible mean of 140.

What's the ratio?

Ratios are a way to compare one thing to another using mathematics. They are usually written in the form

a:b

Making squash

Orange squash comes in concentrated form. To make it drinkable, you add water in a ratio of 1:4. This means that you need four parts of water for every one part of squash.

To make a litre of squash:

Scaling up

Model aeroplane kits allow you to make a model that is exactly the same proportions as the real thing. A popular scale is **1:72**.

Life-size aeroplane

This scale was chosen to make the imperial measurement of **1 inch (about 2.5 cm)** on the model equivalent to exactly **6 feet (1.8 m)** on the real plane. That's about the height of a full-grown man.

1.8 m

Model aeroplane

2.5 cm

1 part
squash
(200 ml
squash)

4 parts
water
(800 ml
water)

5 parts
squash drink
(1 litre squash
drink)

2 metres

1

1

1

3 metres

Thailand

1

1

2

1

1

Flags

National flags are
made using ratios. The
French and Thai flags both
have stripes of blue, white
and red, but the ratios are
very different. The French
national flag has three equal
vertical bands with a 1:1:1
ratio, while the Thai flag has
five horizontal bands with a
1:1:2:1:1 ratio.

Both flags have a
width:length ratio of

2:3

The golden ratio

The golden ratio is a special number, known as phi (φ), that crops up in many places in nature, and has long been used by artists and architects. It describes a proportion that we find balanced and pleasing to look at.

Finding the golden ratio

To find the golden ratio, you need to divide a line such that the longer part divided by the smaller part is equal to the whole line divided by the larger part.

A

B

A+B

$$\frac{A}{B} = \frac{A+B}{A} = 1.618... = \varphi$$

If we make a rectangle using the golden ratio, it looks like this:

Many artists use the golden rectangle shape for their canvasses.

$\varphi = 1.618...$

1

Golden Rectangle

1

Phi can be written as a fraction that goes on forever, like this:

$$\varphi = 1 + \cfrac{1}{1 + \cfrac{1}{1 + \cfrac{1}{1 + ...}}}$$

1

$\varphi = 1.618...$

The golden spiral

A golden rectangle has a special property. Draw a square inside it, and you produce another golden rectangle by its side. You can keep on repeating this to produce ever-smaller golden rectangles. Joining up the corners of each square, you produce a golden spiral:

The Whirlpool galaxy's billions of stars form into golden spirals.

The seeds in a sunflower are arranged in golden spirals.

Perfect pentagrams

A pentagram is the shape of a five-pointed star, which has been used by many human societies as a magical symbol. Does it look like a pleasing shape to you? **Three golden ratios can be found in a pentagram:**

a/b = 1.618
b/c = 1.618
c/d = 1.618

Showing your final results

When faced with a mass of numbers, it can be hard to see patterns and interpret your results. Mathematicians have various ways of displaying their results, using tables, charts and graphs.

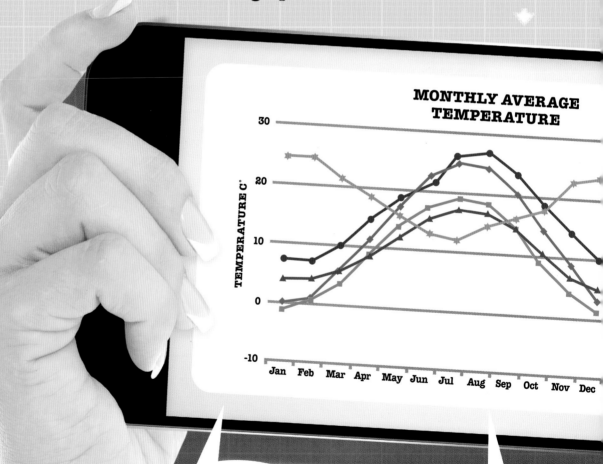

"Brrrr, it's snowing here in London."

"Ha ha, we've just got back from the beach in Sydney!"

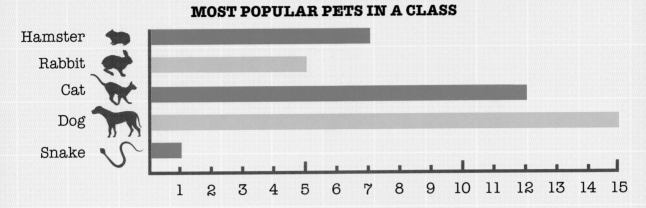

MOST POPULAR PETS IN A CLASS

	1	2	3	4	5	6	7	8	9	10	11	12	13	14	15

Bar and pie charts

Bar charts, like the one above, allow you to quickly compare different quantities. If you arrange this same information in a pie chart, like the one below, you can see easily what proportion of the total number of pets each pet is.

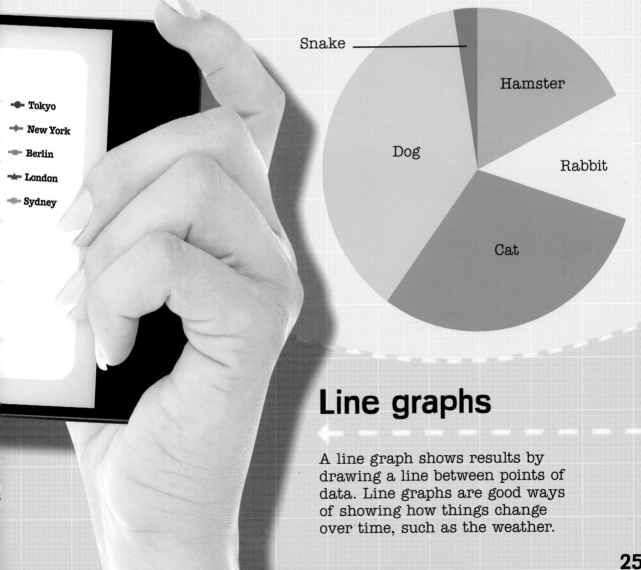

- Tokyo
- New York
- Berlin
- London
- Sydney

Line graphs

A line graph shows results by drawing a line between points of data. Line graphs are good ways of showing how things change over time, such as the weather.

How to run a fair election

Proportional representation

Voters vote for a particular party, which gains the seats represented by its percentage of the vote. In an election, 200 seats are to be filled in parliament. Six parties are standing for election, and they each receive the following percentage of the vote, as shown below:

In a democracy, people are elected to public positions. Those running the election need a system to measure who is the most popular candidate or party, which isn't always as easy as it might sound. These are some of the systems used.

Blue	Red	Orange	Pink	Green	Purple
20%	35%	6%	21%	10%	8%

The parties receive seats according to the percentage of 200 that their vote represents.

Blue 40 seats, **Red** 70 seats, **Orange** 12 seats, **Pink** 42 seats, **Green** 20 seats, **Purple** 16 seats.

To form the government, a party needs a majority of the seats, which means 101 seats or more. No single party has a majority, so after the election, parties form coalitions to make their total up to over 100. For instance, Red and Pink could form a coalition, or Blue, Pink and Green.

Proportional representation is thought by some to be the fairest method of electing a parliament. It normally produces coalition governments.

First past the post

An alternative method is for each seat in parliament to be allocated to a constituency, which is a smaller area. Within each constituency, candidates from each party stand against each other, and the one with the most votes wins. With these results in a single constituency, the Red Party candidate is elected:

Blue	Red	Orange	Pink	Green	Purple
20	35	6	21	10	8

A problem with this method is that a party can win lots of votes and come second in many constituencies without winning any seats, which many think is unfair. Supporters of the system say that it is more likely to produce a clear winner than proportional representation, which makes for stronger governments.

Please don't hate me!

Where just one person is to be elected, such as in a mayoral election, a system called the single transferable vote is often used. Voters rank each candidate in order, from their favourite down to their least favourite. When votes are counted, the least popular candidates are eliminated, and their votes transfered, until a winner is found. In this system, it is important to be liked, but it is just as important not to be hated!

Quiz

1 What **percentage** of these squares is coloured yellow?

a)

1	2	3	4	5	6	7	8	9	10
11	12	13	14	15	16	17	18	19	20
21	22	23	24	25	26	27	28	29	30
31	32	33	34	35	36	37	38	39	40
41	42	43	44	45	46	47	48	49	50
51	52	53	54	55	56	57	58	59	60
61	62	63	64	65	66	67	68	69	70
71	72	73	74	75	76	77	78	79	80
81	82	83	84	85	86	87	88	89	90
91	92	93	94	95	96	97	98	99	100

b)

1	2	3	4	5	6	7	8	9	10
11	12	13	14	15	16	17	18	19	20
21	22	23	24	25	26	27	28	29	30
31	32	33	34	35	36	37	38	39	40
41	42	43	44	45	46	47	48	49	50
51	52	53	54	55	56	57	58	59	60

c)

| 1 | 2 | 3 | 4 | 5 | 6 | 7 | 8 |

2 Express each of the above percentages as a **fraction** in its simplest form.

3 Rolling **two fair dice**, what are the chances of rolling

a) **double 1**

b) **3 and 4**

c) **a total of 10 or more**

4 In a lottery, you win the jackpot if you choose **six numbers out of 49 correctly.** You are watching the draw take place, and your first five numbers all come up. **What are the chances** that you will win the jackpot when the **last ball** is drawn?

5 In three coin tosses, what are the chances of throwing **two heads** and **a tail?**

28

6 You choose **two cards** at random from a standard deck. What are the chances that they are both the **same suit?**

7 Look at these exam results for a maths class.

83 42 55 69 12 94 65

a) What is the **mean average** score?

b) What is the **median score**?

8 a) What is the **mode** out of these numbers?

2 4 3 3 5 6 5 3 7 3

b) If you choose a number **at random** from the list, what are the chances that it will be the **mode value**?

9 A model aircraft is made to a scale of **1:50**. If its wingspan in real life is **20 metres**, what will be the wingspan of the model in centimetres?

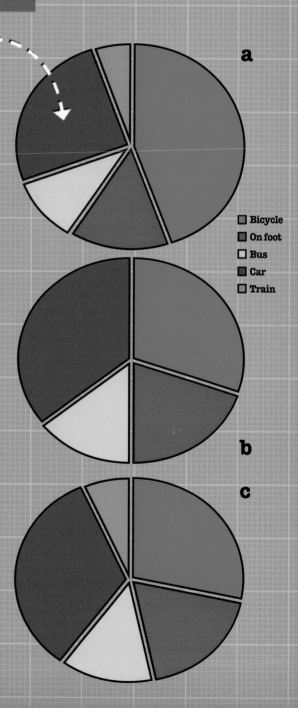

10 This is the flag of Spain. The proportions of the stripes are in the **ratio 1:2:1**. The proportions of the width to length are in the **ratio 2:3**. What are the measurements of **a** and **b**?

11 We asked **60 children** how they travelled to school. The answers were as follows: **Bicycle 17, On foot 11, Bus 8, Car 20, Train 4**. Which pie chart shows this correctly?

12 In an election using the proportional representation system, the following percentage votes were won by each party: **Blue 5, Red 11, Orange 33, Pink 36, Green 15** The two largest parties, Orange and Pink, are asked to try to form a coalition government with at least **51%** of the vote. They refuse to form a coalition with each other, and want to form coalitions with as few other parties as possible.

a) What **coalitions** could the parties form that would give them a **majority**?
b) If the Blue party refuses to ally with the Red party and the Green party refuses to ally with the Orange party, **which coalition** will be formed?

□ Bicycle
□ On foot
□ Bus
▨ Car
□ Train

Glossary

Bar chart
A way of displaying results in which the length of the bar shows the number of times each value occurs.

False positive
A result in a medical test that suggests that a patient has a disease or condition when they do not have it.

Golden ratio
A special ratio between two lengths, in which dividing the sum of the lengths by the longer length produces the same number as dividing the longer length by the shorter length. Also called phi (φ), it is equal to approximately 1.618.

Line graph
A way of displaying results in which each data point is connected to the one next to it by a straight line. A line graph can be useful to see how a value changes over time.

Mean
An average that is found by adding a series of values together then dividing by the number of values.

Median
An average that is the middle value of a series of values arranged in order. Half the remaining values are larger than the median and half are smaller.

Mode
An average that is the most common value in a series of values.

Payout
In a lottery, the percentage of the total amount paid for tickets that is given out in prize money.

Percentage
A fraction that is expressed in terms of parts per one hundred.

Pie chart
A way of displaying data in which the total number of values is represented by a circle, and the proportion of the total for each separate value is represented by a sector in the circle.

Probability
The chance that something will happen. Probabilities can be expressed in various ways: as a fraction between 0 and 1; as a ratio of the number of times the thing will happen to the number of times it will not happen; or as a percentage. For instance, the chance of throwing a head with a fair coin toss can be written as ½, 1:1 or 50%.

Proportional representation
A way of running an election in which each party receives seats in a parliament according to the percentage of the vote they receive.

Range
The difference between the largest and smallest values in a set of values.

Ratio
A way of comparing one quantity with another.

Index

Answers

1. a) 20% b) 40% c) 75%
2. a) $^1/_5$ b) $^2/_5$ c) $^3/_4$
3. a) $^1/_{36}$ b) $^1/_{18}$ c) $^1/_6$
4. There is a $^1/_{44}$ chance that your sixth number will be drawn, so the chance of winning the jackpot is $^1/_{44}$.
5. There are three different ways you can do this: Tail first, Tail second or Tail third. Overall, there are 2 × 2 × 2 possible combinations, so the chance of two heads and a tail is $^3/_8$

6. There are 13 of each suit in the deck. Whichever card you pick first, there are now 12 of the same suit left in a pack of 51 cards. So the chance that both cards are the same suit is $^{12}/_{51}$.
7. a) 60 b) 65
8. a) The mode is 3. b) 3 occurs 4 times out of 10, so the chance of picking the mode is $^4/_{10}$, or $^2/_5$
9. 20 m = 2,000 cm; 2,000 ÷ 50 = 40 cm
10. a) 2 m b) 6 m
11. c)
12. a) Pink/Green; Pink/Red/Blue; Orange/Green/Red; Orange/Green/Blue b) Pink/Green